THE McSQAW GANG

by

Chloe Tuten

The McSqaw Gang

2022 Copyright © by Chloe Tuten

ISBN: 978-1-63073-403-9

Published by:
Faithful Life Publishers
North Fort Myers, FL 33903

888.720.0950 • info@FaithfulLifePublishers.com
FaithfulLifePublishers.com

Front cover credit: Emily Johnson (photographer),
Magnus/Morgan/Miles/Phineas/Elijah/Sydney
(The Gang)

Published in the United States of America
25 24 23 22 21   1 2 3 4 5

THIS IS HOW WE KNOW WHAT LOVE
IS: THAT JESUS CHRIST LAID DOWN
HIS LIFE FOR US. 1 John 3:16

Chapter 1

A long, deserted, side street in New York
City was almost entirely dark. For all its
streetlights, saving one, had been smashed
by the large rocks that lay underneath
them. But the one light—that had escaped
destruction—shone bravely on, showing up
all it could, including three dark shadows
that were slipping along the side of the street
toward it. Reaching it, the first shadow
materialized into a young man by stepping
directly under it and giving a peculiar
whistle. The two other shadows joined the
first and they assumed the waiting attitude,
of standing with their hands in their pockets,
tapping the ground with their shoes.

"ShawShank said they'd be here early," said the second shadow. A skinny, five foot, seven-inch-tall young man, with black hair, in the military high and tight, and light blue eyes.

"Something's happened, it would just be nice to know what," answered the first young man, who looked the same as the second, except that his eyes were a brighter blue.

"And Curtly, where do you think he's got himself?" growled the third young man, the spitting image of the other two but with dark blue eyes and a fierce look on his face. The three of them were wearing tennis shoes, jeans, white T-shirts, and brown leather jackets.

"He found some kind of day job working for some young man," answered the first.

The third gave him a quick look, from under his dark eyebrows, "What sort of young man?"

"I don't know, he seemed pretty talkative."

The third glared at him, "Why didn't you find out?"

"How was I supposed to?! Walk up to him and ask him if he's a good man, or if he likes to traffic or rape young boys?"

"Then why did you let Temp work for 'im?"

"Temple's got to eat sometime and work's the only way you can do that. And no, I couldn't stay with him cause the guy wanted him to write something for 'im and I don't know how to write."

"There he is," sighed the second young man, looking with relief at a dark form approaching them. The light, when he reached it, showed him to be a five-foot, three-inch, strongly built young man, dressed just like the others. With buzz cut white-blond hair, and light brown eyes.

"How'd the man you worked for today, treat you?" asked the third, glaring at Temple.

"Very well. He was a really nice man."

"I don't trust nice men, they always have a reason for being nice. Don't go near him again without one of us."

"Yes, Daris."

Two young people now stepped out into the light, behind the four friends, with the silence of alley cats. They were dressed the same as the others except that they were barefoot, and they looked exactly alike. Both were super thin, with light brown hair cut to their jaw line, dark brown eyes, and very beautiful, girly faces. They were five foot and five inches tall.

"Hey, ShawShank," said the second, noticing them.

"Hey Darn," answered the one on the left, in a strong tenor.

"What happened?" asked the first.

"A delay," the left boy answered.

"What sort of delay?" asked the first.

"A sort."

"What—?"

"Don't ask," interrupted Daris, "We all know ShawShank don't talk about their personal affairs."

"How was the man you worked with today, Temp?" asked the left boy, "Was he good to you?"

"Yes."

"Good. How about the Porr gang, they made any advances?"

"No," said the first. "And you, why were you *going* to be early?"

"Because we were. But there's a new gang we've been watching that's coming to town. We'll work on finding out its name. They say the leader of it is Draygon McSqaw."

"Who's Draygon McSqaw?" asked Temple.

"He's a race car driver," answered the left boy, "Doesn't do the big races. Hardly anybody knows about 'im. We've seen him once."

"All of you," Temple asked, glancing at the others, "Or just you and Shaw?"

"I've seen him," said the first, "Once."

"You've seen everything, Dick," said Temple, "Why don't the three of you stick together more, like ShawShank do? Are triplets not as close as twins?"

"We're as close as we're ever goin' to be," said Daris.

"You don't have to never leave each other's side to be close," said the first, otherwise known as Dick.

"We're close," said Darn, "Just in a different way than ShawShank."

"You like ours better, don't you?" said the left boy, Shank, with a grin.

"Of course he does," said Darn, "Cause that's how his family always did things. And that's okay. It's fine to like what you're used to."

"Are we planning on crashing some time or does talking give you guys all the rest you need for tomorrow?" asked Shaw, the right twin, in an alto, folding his arms across his chest.

"Sure it does," said Daris, "And if you'd join in it, you could be as refreshed as the rest of us."

"Then I much prefer to be quiet."

"Oh, quit it," said Dick, "Come on, it's time we crashed."

He led the way up the street, then turned into a dark alley. When they had gone twelve feet into it, they lay down. Dick lay against Darn's back, Darn against Daris' back, Daris against Temple's, Temple against Shaw and--after Shank had taken off his jacket and laid it over Shaw's legs--he laid down with Shaw at his back.

Dick raised his voice and prayed, "Dear Jesus, thank You for this day, for helping us through it. Thank You for work and food. Please give us a good night's sleep and prepare us for tomorrow. Thank You for Your love and what it does to us. Thank You for making us into the men You want us to be. I pray *Jesus* over us tonight, Your power and Your protection, Lord. And I bind all the spiritual forces of wickedness in heavenly places, in the Name and authority of Jesus. In Jesus' Name, Amen."

The boys all closed their eyes and were soon asleep.

Chapter 2

It was night again.

The triplets, Temple and Shank were walking along the side of a street that still had most of its lights working.

"So where did you say Shaw was?" asked Dick turning to Shank.

"I didn't say."

"Where is he then?"

"Where he is. But I found out the name of the gang that's coming to town. It would definitely fit McSqaw."

"What is it?" asked Temple.

"The Scar gang. Sounds like some real nice people to meet doesn't it?"

"No," said Temple, "Why does it fit McSqaw?"

"Cause he's got scars all over," said Dick, "Race car drivers can get into more than they bargained for, in wrecks."

"You can't scare me," said Daris, looking at his brother, "Let 'em bring it on."

"What's he talking about?" Temple asked.

"His one ambition," said Dick, "Of all the things in the world he could be, he wants to race cars."

"Why?"

"Because," said Daris, with a grim smile, "You can speed and fight without getting put in jail for it. And you can give all you got to win."

Temple nodded and looked down at his shoes. As they turned onto the street with only one light, Temple looked back up at Dick, "Why don't we have a name?"

Dick stared at him, "I have a name. It's Dick Carmen."

"No. I mean a gang name."

Dick opened his mouth and then shut it, as a beautiful alto voice rang out, into the quiet street:

"Slowly, gently,
night unfurls its splendor.
Grasp it, sense it,
tremulous and tender.

"Hearing is believing,
Music is deceiving,
hard as lightning,
soft as candlelight.

"Dare you trust
the music of the night.

"Close your eyes
for your eyes will only tell you the truth,
and the truth isn't what you want to see!

"In the dark
it is easy to pretend—
that the truth is what it ought to be."

("*The Music of The Night*" by Mr. Andrew
Lloyd Webber)

A dark figure stepped directly under the
one light, far in front of them, and began in
a rich tenor,

"Sing once again with me
a strange duet.
My power over you
grows strong again.

"And though you turn from me
to glance behind,
The phantom of the opera is there
inside your mind."

Then the alto voice sang,

"Those who have seen your face
draw back in fear
I am the mask you wear,"

Then the tenor,

"It's me they hear."

Then together:

"My spirit and your voice
in one combined,"

Alto:

"The phantom of the opera is here.
Inside my mind."

Tenor:

"In all your phantasy you always knew,
that man and mystery"

Alto:

> "Are both in you."

Together:

> "And in this flattery,
> where night is blind—
> The phantom of the opera is here."

Alto:

> "Inside my mind."

("*The Phantom Of The Opera*" by Mr. Andrew Lloyd Webber)

The figure under the lamp raised his hands and clapped loudly. The boys had come rapidly up to where the alto should be. Shaw stepped out of the darkness and stood with them at the edge of the lamplight, they all stared at the figure before them. He stood at six foot, with short, sandy colored hair, slicked back from his face with lots of grease, and nicely combed. He was slender, just like they were, had beautiful green eyes and a tantalizing smile. He was truly movie-star handsome.

"Why, you're a boy!" he exclaimed, staring at Shaw, "That's amazing! You have a really good voice! I work for a movie production company and I have only ever met one boy that could sing like that. It's very rare."

"Which makes you common place," returned Shaw.

The movie star grinned; "I suppose so."

"You're the man I wrote stuff for yesterday," said Temple, "Why are you here?"

"Trying to find a good place to sleep."

"Why? Don't you make a lot of money?"

"I make pretty good money, but I have other ways to spend it."

"What ways?" asked Daris.

"Clothes, food, etc."

"What's the etc.?" asked Shank, "Your clothes cost as much as ours do and you don't look like you eat any more than we do, so what do you do?"

The movie star looked at them all in silence for a moment, then said, "I have an old dad whose got a lot of really special care needs. So I have him in an upper class nursing home and I hire experts—in his field of needs—to work with him every day. And I'm not anywhere near being a famous movie star, cause the company's not that big, so that's where all my money goes."

"You must have a really good dad," said Shank in disbelief.

"Actually, I don't even know him. He never married my mom, so when he found out she was pregnant with me and she wasn't going to have an abortion, he left her never to return. Just a year ago I ran across him in the street. He has Alzheimer's so he thought I was my mother and started yelling at me. After I found out who he was I figured I should do him a good turn, cause I had absolutely nothing to do with my money anyway. Mom had died and I had no other relatives, so it worked out."

"Why in the world would you do that for a man who did that to you?" asked Shank, "You don't look old enough to have that kind of character."

"God had to do that for me in a very real way, not only on the cross but in my personal life. And once He's done it for you,

you can't help but want others to know how it feels."

"So you're a saint or you think you are," said Daris, sarcastically.

The movie star laughed, "No. I got plenty of personal reasons not to think myself a saint. I'm just Jesus-covered Dean, Dean Myles. It's been a pleasure to meet you all. Goodnight."

He strode across the street and laid down against the old wall of a building, standing opposite the one remaining streetlight. Dick led the others up the street and into their alley.

"We'll keep a watch tonight just for kicks," said Dick, "I'll take the first."

The others laid down in their chest to back positions and--after Shank had laid his jacket over Shaw's legs--Darn prayed over them and they fell asleep. All except Dick, who sat staring into the night.

Chapter 3

Loud laughter, coming down the alley from the opposite side then the one they came in by, made Dick jump to his feet. Darn and Shaw, who were light sleepers, sprang to theirs in an instant. Their motion woke Daris and Shank who leaped to their feet. Daris, his sleep filled mind, realizing that people were coming, knelt down, shook Temple awake, and helped him to his feet.

"What is it?" Asked Temple, then caught his breath, "The Porr gang!"

The full moon was just at the right angle to cast a brilliant light over the five young men and three young women approaching them.

"Who's the eighth boy," whispered Temple, "I thought there was only seven of them."

"There are," said Daris "He's a new guy."

"I've never seen him before," said Shank.

"I have."

The boys spun round and found themselves face to face with Dean Myles. He wasn't looking at them, but beyond them, into the face of the mysterious gangster.

"Hey, Johnathan," he said quietly, stepping forward, "Long time no see."

Johnathan—a young man with three scars that trailed from just below his right eye down to his jawline—stared back at him, "Who are you?"

"I'm the boy that gave you those scars and I advise you and your friends, if you don't want some more of the same, not to mess with us."

Johnathan's scared face twisted into a quiet smile, "I've wanted to meet you again ever since that day. And now I find you're only a pretty kid whose strength came from his mama's nursing strings, which he refused to let go of. Rather than from his own arm. Bring on some more scars if your tiny arm won't break trying to make them. This should be fun."

Dean's eyes glittered like the green water of a dark pool when the sun shines on it. He wasn't smiling any more. His lips were pressed into a firm line. He slowly clenched his hands. The two closed the distance between them and began to walk in a small circle between the two gangs. On the third circle as Dean was passing in front of the Porr gang, one of the girls sprang forward and caught him round the neck. Johnathan swung. But Dean—reacting instantly— reached for the girl's arms, at the same time giving Johnathan a powerful kick in the groin. Johnathan's arm missed its mark and he fell to his knees, holding himself. The Porr gang closed around Dean at the same time Daris, with a mighty "Yeah!"

led the others forward in a rush. And the battle was joined. Daris tackled everybody and anybody biting and pounding. Dick preferred to grab your swinging fists and kick you. Darn slugged as hard as he could but seemed especially made for a punching bag and ended up getting clobbered. Still, from his-flat on his back-position on the ground, he would yank your legs out from under you and then punch you. Not seeming to care how many times you hit him back. ShawShank seemed to always be moving, slipping in and out of the ranks of fighters, and nearly always hitting you in the places it hurts worst to be hit. Temple quickly joined Darn on the ground, but instead of punching you after he'd pulled you down, he bit you wherever and as hard as he could. To Dean, the whole thing seemed to be a wild, intricate, speed dance. He never stopped twisting, writhing, and folding. He hit you with everything he had, elbows, arms, hands, hips, knees, feet, head-all of it. And wherever he hit you it felt like you'd come in contact with stinging steel. The Porr gang—a bunch of lean, hard, twenty-year olds—though they fought like wild beasts, quickly found themselves losing ground and began falling back.

"I'll have my gang give you a whipping you'll never forget if you yield an inch!" roared Johnathan, who was locked in a horrible fight with Dean. He was stronger, but Dean was good at dodging, and kept him twisted up in knots with all his moves. The Porr gang threw themselves back at the boys, with everything in them. Johnathan and Dean got separated as did ShawShank. Shank found himself fighting two of the girls while Dean got stuck with Matt, the cold, thin, iron-like leader of the Porr gang. Shaw found himself fighting Johnathan. But the boys quickly fought off the Porr gang's second onslaught. Johnathan, enraged, whipped out his knife. Shank saw it flash toward Shaw and screamed, "Knife!" But there was no time, and he hadn't been able to free himself from the clutches of the last girl. Dean also saw, but he was arms and legs involved with Matt. Johnathan was much bigger than Shaw and held him fully engaged with just one arm and both his legs. Instead of stabbing him in the side, Johnathan raised his knife and plunged it down towards his skinny, white neck. Dean threw his head in the way and the knife sank threw his cheek. Just then, Shaw gathered all his strength and rammed his knee into Johnathan's gut. Johnathan lost his hold on the knife and fell to his knees. Darn yanked Matt's legs out from under him and Dean was able to wrench himself away from his fallen opponent. And get out of the fight long enough to pull the knife out of his cheek, hurling it against the faraway wall of a building. He darted back into the fight but the Porr gang were already in full flight. Johnathan held his ground a little longer, calling out, "My gang will whip you cowards!"

Then he too turned and raced down the alley. The boys did not chase them but watched until they were swallowed up in darkness.

Chapter 4

Everyone but Dean joined Temple and Darn on the ground. Dean gathered several large rocks, spitting blood out of his mouth while he did so. Then he came and sat down with them. He lifted one from his lap and held its freezing surface against his cheek.

"So," said Daris, staring at Dean, "You slept here on purpose cause you knew they were comin'."

"I knew they would be doin' their stuff in this part of town and that Temple lived somewhere in this area. So I figured I might as well sleep on this street, as any other, cause everything I told you is true," said Dean, stopping to spit out blood whenever it gathered in his mouth.

"How do you know Johnathan?" asked Shank.

"Who is Johnathan?" asked Shaw.

Dean looked at ShawShank, his eyes looked like the dark green water at the bottom of an ocean. They wandered away and stared down the alley. Still staring away from them, Dean began in a low voice.

"On my sixteenth birthday, mom came down with some kind of bug, so I told her to stay at home and rest, then I went off to work. We had to work late that night, finishing filming a production. When I got home, I found that four guys had broken into our apartment. Johnathan was still in the act of raping my mother when I came in, the others had already done so. The next few minutes are a blur in my memory. But I distinctly remember ripping Johnathan's face, tearing into it with all I had. Suddenly, I found myself standing alone in the room. I could hear the heavy thud of their feet as they ran down the stairs. I stared down at my burning hands. My fingernails were caked with flesh, my hands covered with blood. Their blood, cause I wasn't bleeding at all. But I didn't care what my hands looked like or what I had done with them. It was what lay behind me that mattered. I was so afraid to turn, but I had too, for her sake. She was dead. I tried everything I knew to bring her back, but it was of no use. I sat on my knees staring down at her mulled body for I don't know how long. Somebody started laughing real loud in the apartment next to ours and I just couldn't take it anymore. I ran away from everything, and plunged, heart and soul, into drugs. I never really knew what I was doing. Until one morning, I woke up in the hands of the police and served six months in jail-for raping a young girl while high on drugs. I had just done—to a young girl—the thing that had killed my mother and ruined my life. This realization is what put me on my face, at the feet of Jesus. My mother was a Christian and had taught me to be one. But I never made her faith, my faith, so when suffering came, it did nothing for me. I had blamed God. Now I saw it was us, Johnathan and me, that were to blame. But my mother had said, Jesus had taken all the blame, on the cross, for us. We just had to except that to be saved. So I did. When I got out, I got my job back and here I am. There's no vengeance in me anymore, but when I heard the scar gang was comin' to town, I figured I'd keep an eye on them. I don't want anyone comin' home to what I did. And I don't want any little kids gettin' hurt like I hurt that girl."

"Did you ever try to find out what happened to her?" asked Shank.

"Yes."

"What happened?" Shank's dark brown eyes keenly searched Dean's face.

"She had an abortion and a hysterectomy, and nearly died. But, after being in the hospital nearly six months, she left, leaving no trace as to where."

"Why did you try to find her?" asked Shaw.

"To see if she was ok and if I could do anything in reparation."

"How old was she?" asked Shank.

"Fourteen."

"Did she have any family?" asked Shaw.

"I don't know."

There was a long silence after this. Dean laid down the hot, bloody rock he'd been holding against his cheek, picked up one of the cold ones in his lap, and held it against his cheek. Dick laid down. The others, excepting Dean, followed his example. The triplets and Temple were soon breathing regularly in sleep but the ShawShank watched Dean, from under their half-closed lids. As he sat motionless, pressing a stone to his cheek, his deep green eyes staring off into the darkness.

Chapter 5

Shaw woke with a start and sat up. Shank sat up beside him and flashed a weary grin. They both looked over at Dean. He hadn't moved from his place and sat slumped forward in sleep. ShawShank looked over at the others, they were all lost in dreamland.

"That was a close call with that knife," said Shank, staring his brother straight in the eyes.

"Sorry. I just found myself fighting him."

"Of course," said Shank, unconvinced.

"It was nice of Dean to take it," said Shaw, "It might cause a disfigurement that may ruin his career.

"You're being evasive," said Shank, quietly, never letting his brother's eyes wander from his. Shaw glared at him and neither of them spoke a word. They both started at a quick drawn breath to their right and looked over as Dean raised his head. His face was ghastly white, dried blood covered his right cheek and his greasy, sandy colored hair was all messed up. But he shook himself, looked over at them and grinned his tantalizing smile—though he winced at the pain it brought to his cheek, "Good morning."

"Good morning," ShawShank answered.

"Well," said Dean, after an awkward silence.

"Since Johnathan didn't come back last night, we won't see him again til tonight. So I I'll drop by the hospital and get myself stitched up before I go to work. I'll be back tonight to help you fight' em," and he stood up.

"You think he'll come back?" asked Shaw.

"Oh, I know he will," said Dean, "And he'll bring the whole scar gang with him. They will want to ground us into powder for our audacity yesterday."

"We could sleep somewhere else," said Temple, who had woken without anyone noticing.

"They'd hunt us into another state if they had too," said Dean.

"How do you know?" Temple asked.

"The way Johnathan answered me last night," said Dean, "He's never forgiven' me for ripping up his face and now he's found me—and with you—he'll have the gang take it out on all of us."

"Does the gang really obey him?" asked Temple.

"No, I don't think so. But their leader and two others raped my mother with Johnathan, and I whipped them all. So I'm sure they'll have their score to pay off too and the scar gang *listens to* their leader."

"So this *was* about vengeance for you," said Shank, "Cause you just made it ten times harder for us."

"Would you have been able to fight off the Porr gang and Johnathan without me?" asked Dean, quietly.

"Maybe, said Shank.

"I'm sorry then," said Dean, "I was wrong in my judgement of how strong you were. Will you please forgive me?"

Shaw sprang to his feet, "No. We won't. You saved my life. Shank would have a dead brother if you hadn't been there. He should be the one apologizing for his attitude. I thank you," and he held out his hand.

Dean gripped and shook it, heartily.

"Your brother's probably right, though," he said, "If I hadn't been there it would have changed the way the battle looked. Maybe Johnathan wouldn't have fought so well if he hadn't been mad at me first. I'm sorry. I tend to think of something that looks right and go do it, without giving it the second thought it needs. Please forgive me."

"No." Shaw flashed.

Dean looked from defiant Shaw to glaring Shank.

"Well," he said, looking over at Temple, "Goodbye."

And he strode off.

"I don't trust him," said Shank.

"Well, I do," said Shaw.

Chapter 6

"He won't come," said Shank.

"Yes, he will," said Shaw.

Shank shook his head, "Nope."

"Yep," said Shaw, nodding his.

The six of them stood under the lamp that worked, in the dark street.

"I've never seen you disagree before," said Temple.

"Yes well, Shaw tends to be a sensible young man, most of the time," said Shank.

"And Shank tends to be a noble young man, most of the time," said Shaw.

ShawShank glared at each other.

Then Shank turned on the others, "Seriously, who thinks Dean is going to come back?"

"I do," said Dick, "I mean, why would he tell us his whole story and all the bad things he's done if he hasn't really changed. What could he gain by it? I think he honestly wants to help us."

"I think he'll come, too," said Temple.

"What about you Darn, Daris?" asked Shank.

Darn shook his head, "He's a movie star. We could get killed tonight—Johnathan would have killed Shaw. And yes, Dean saved Shaw, but that was a good guy's instant reaction. If he comes back, after a day of thought and stitches, he's crazy. Cause if he doesn't die with us his beauty will probably be so marred the production company won't take him back. He could lose everything—for what?"

"He ain't comin," said Daris, "Not a chance."

"See," said Shank, turning back to his brother.

"He'll be here soon," said Shaw.

"Yes, he will, is everyone ready?" asked Dean, stepping into the light. Everyone jumped, spun round, and took a deep breath.

"I told you so," said Shaw, ramming Shank in the side with his elbow.

"Told him what?" asked Dean.

"Doesn't matter," said Dick, "We're ready."

"Good, cause there's sixteen of 'em," said Dean,

"I didn't know they were that big."

"And there's only seven of us," said Temple.

"The perfect amount," said Dean, "Cause seven is the number of completion.

"That could be our name!" cried Temple, turning to Dick, "The Complete gang!"

They were all silent.

"Um, keep tryin' kid," said Daris.

"Shhh," said Darn, "Listen."

They listened; the thud of many feet sounded distant but clear.

The Carmans, Dean Myles, Temple Curtly and ShawShank, took off their jackets and dropped them behind the light pole. Then they moved closer together and stood tense, facing in the direction of the sounds.

Dick began to pray aloud, "Lord Jesus, into your hands we commit ourselves and those who come against us. Do your will with us, Lord. Please save them and lay not this sin to their charge. Thank you for this night and for giving us each other. We love you. In Jesus' name," and they all said, "Amen."

Johnathan and three others emerged from the dark alley, where the boys usually slept, and stocked toward them. The rest of the Scar gang followed and spread out, till they all came on side by side. The light showed them up well. They were hoods.

Chapter 7

Joshua Johnston, the young man, farthest to the right, who had come out beside Johnathan, was powerfully made. With thick, heavily greased, dark brown hair. He stood at six foot, five, with black eyes and a short, thick beard that covered his bottom jaw and upper lip. A large, white scar ran from his left cheek bone, straight up, into his hair, where it was lost to view. And he looked to be about twenty-two years of age.

Johnathan Hanks walked beside him. He was an inch shorter and not so muscular. He had sandy hair and dark blue eyes and no facial hair to speak of. He was twenty-one.

Beside him, was a five-foot, three-inch, thirty-one-year-old, with a huge chest and a hunk of muscle on each arm. He had a bald head, beady brown eyes and a bushy, brown beard. His scar ran from his left eyebrow, up, across his tattooed scalp and down into the nape of his neck. This was Arthur Waldon.

Next to him was thirty-four-year-old Jacob. Not much bigger than a light pole in size, he stood at six foot, three. His hair laid like dead, white flakes on his head. And his light blue eyes were sunken into his face, which was long and skinny. His scar ran from one ear, over his nose to the other ear.

A six-foot, seven-inch, thirty-seven-year-old, giant stocked beside him. Everything about Dunce was big, His leg muscles, his arm muscles, his chest muscles, his neck muscles. His head, ears, eyes, nose, and mouth—everything. A big scar ran from the bottom of his right ear, along his neck, to his left shoulder.

Beside him, stepped a beautiful, white faced girl of eighteen. Dawn Carter was slender and stood at five foot, seven. She had bright blue eyes, red lips and blond hair. But the ends of her hair, which was cut just below her shoulders, had been dyed the color of blood. And a scar ran from the middle of her left ear, to her jawline.

Next to her strode a powerful woman of twenty-four. Her black hair was cut in a bob, her gray eyes looked as impassible as steel and her light pink lips were set in a firm line. Dara Peters scar went from her left eyebrow, across her nose to her right jawline. And she was five feet, five inches tall.

At her side walked a five foot, eight, thin, twenty-nine-year-old, African American. Thick dreadlocks fell to his waist and from the middle of his forehead to the end of his nose, lay a white scar. His name was Michael Huston.

The forty-five-year-old, African American, beside him, looked much stronger than he and wore a full beard. A white scar encircled Eric Matthews entire right eye. And he was the same height as the two white men beside him, five feet, nine- inches.

Thirty-six-year-old James beside him, was just as big, with curly, light brown hair and a waxed mustache. He had dark blue eyes and a scar from his upper lip down to the end of his chin.

The skinny thirty-year-old beside him had a pink mohawk, with the rest of his head shaved. Tatts up and down both arms and a fleshy two-inch scar on his right cheek. He was John.

Next to him was a wiry, forty-seven-year-old, with orange hair, green eyes, and a profusion of freckles. Caleb Conner's scar went from the end of one ear, over his mouth, to the end of the other. He was five foot, eight.

Beside him was a girl, five feet and four inches, tall. Her incredibly curly, sandy colored hair was drawn into a tight ponytail at the top of her head. A scar ran from the left corner of her mouth to her jaw and her face was stern and sharp. She—Sheryl, and the girl beside her, were stick thin and had soft brown eyes. Sheryl was seventeen, and the five-foot, two-inch Sherry was sixteen.

Sherry's curly hair had been forced into a French braid, that hung between her shoulder blades. Her sweet gentle face was marred by the two-inch, jagged scar on her right cheek.

Jeff Marcus the nineteen-year-old boy at her side, stood at five foot eleven. With light brown hair hanging to his shoulders and light blue eyes. He was powerfully built, with a scar from his right nostril to down to the right corner of his mouth.

But the African American twenty-year-old beside him was massive. Tom Martin was six foot one, had short, grizzly hair and beard, and a one-inch scar on his left cheek bone.

The whole gang was wearing tank tops, jeans, and Tena-shoes.

Temple's eyes were big as he whispered to Daris, "Which one's McSqaw?"

"He's not here," whispered Dick.

"But Dean said he'd be."

"Dean doesn't get everything right," whispered Daris.

"He probably thought beating up a handful 'u kids already heavily outnumbered and outmatched wouldn't be any fun," whispered Darn.

"Hush mumble boxes!" Snapped Shank, "It's not time to waste our energy talking."

The Scar gang reached them and without a word leaped on them. It was a fierce but short battle, sixteen against seven was just too much. The Scar gang held the boys down and began to beat the living snot out of them. One by one, the boys lost consciousness.

All except Daris, who lay writhing under the not *too* light fists of Michael and Eric. Finally, Michael, the one with the dreadlocks, whipped out his knife and, while Eric held Daris down, seized his hand and cut it off. Daris screamed. Michael put his knife up and went to slug him in the face. When he was yanked up by the hair and given a stunning blow to the right side of his head, that felled him to the earth. He did not rise. The man holding Daris started up, with a muttered imprecation of surprise. But was caught full in the face by the fist that had felled his friend. He fell straight backward and didn't move.

Daris' vision was fuzzy and fading quickly, but he saw the man who'd saved him for one instant. He was six feet, two inches tall, and dressed in a short sleeved, black, skintight T-shirt, and jeans. He was thin but had a muscular chest and powerful arms. Scars lay criss crossed over his face. His short, rich brown hair was well greased, and his eyes were gray. Daris heard the startled cries of the scar gang as they leaped to their feet, "McSqaw! Curse the nosy fiend!"

And then he blacked out.

Chapter 8

"But McSqaw's their leader, why would he fight his own gang?" asked Temple.

The Carmans, ShawShank and Curtly were sitting up. The scar gang was gone.

"Maybe you heard wrong," said Shank.

"Nope," said Daris, "They said, 'McSqaw. Curse the nosy fiend.' "

"Who else could it be?" said Dick.

"Maybe he's just nicer than the rest of them," said Shaw.

"But Dean said he raped his mom with Johnathan," said Dick, "So perhaps he was mad at them for something else."

"I never said Draygon McSqaw raped my mom," said Dean, opening his eyes and sitting up with difficulty (They were all black, blue and red with the bruises and cuts that were everywhere on their bodies).

"I said the Scar gang leader and two others, raped her."

"But Draygon is the Scar gang's leader," said Temple.

Dean stared at him with as much of his eyes as he could open, "Where'd you get that from?"

"Shank."

Shank looked at Dean defiantly, "Did I hear wrong?"

"Um, did you know McSqaw has a lot of scars on his face?"

"Yes," said Shank.

"From race car driving," said Dick.

"That's funny," said Dean, "Because McSqaw's never gotten hurt in a race."

"Your point?" said Shank.

"On my fourteenth birthday, mom took me to McSqaw's first race. He was racing against a Mr. Johnston and a few others. Mr. Johnston was going to go bankrupt if he didn't win. McSqaw won and Mr. Johnston's son found his father dead by his own hand, the next morning. McSqaw had gone the very day of the race and bought a brand-new car with the money he'd earned. Mr. Johnston's son, Joshua, after finding his father with his brains blown out, got in his dad's truck and took off. Both he and McSqaw ended up opposite each other at a four way stop. It was McSqaw's turn to go, so he went. Joshua put on the gas and rammed right into him. McSqaw went to the hospital and Joshua went to jail. Somehow, Joshua's mother was able to get him pardoned. But not before he'd gotten hurt in some fights with his jail companions. Both he and McSqaw entered the world again with facial scars. One became a Christian, started goin' to church and helpin' people. The other became the leader of the Scar gang and raped my mother two years later. I think I can safely say that Draygon McSqaw is not a friend of the Scar gang."

"How did you find out all that?" asked Shank.

"Oh, it was all over the news after the race."

"Do you know Draygon McSqaw, personally?" asked Dick.

"No. I've never seen him. Only his car."

Shaw's head turned quickly, the rest of them followed his gaze and looked down the street. Draygon McSqaw was approaching them. He looked as beat up as they did. They kept silent as he came up. He was carrying eight little bread rolls.

He threw them each one with the words, "You can pay me back when you don't look like spotted red skins," and turned away.

"Hey! Won't you eat with us," said Dean, scrambling to his feet.

Draygon turned, "Sure."

"I'm Dean Myles," said Dean, "It's nice to finally meet you. I was at your first race."

"Draygon McSqaw," said Draygon, gripping Deans proffered hand.

They both sat down. Draygon shut his eyes, bowed his head and was quiet for a moment. They all followed his example. When they raised their heads, he was munching his roll down.

"Thanks for helping us out last night," said Dick.

"You're welcome."

Then they ate quietly, until every crumb was gone.

"How did you know about us and the scar gang," asked Daris.

"I've had some dealings with them in the past. When I heard they were moving to the same town as me I figure' I'd keep an eye on 'em."

"You fought all sixteen of them off us," said Temple.

"Yes."

"Do you know them all?" asked Dean.

"Yes."

"How did you fight them all?" asked Temple, after a pause.

"They'd worn themselves out taking care of you, so they didn't have much left to spend on me."

Dean put his head on one side and scanned Draygon's torn up face, neck, and arms. Daris cocked an eyebrow.

"I got to get to work," said Draygon, standing up, "It was an honor meeting you all."

"But you didn't meet them," said Dean.

Draygon looked at Dean, then turned to the others. "Do you want me to know your names?"

The boys looked at each other and shrugged.

"My name's Dick Carman," said Dick.

"My name's Darn Carman."

"I'm Daris Carman."

"We're triplets," explained Dick.

"I'm Temple Curtly," said Temple.

"Shank."

"Shaw."

"It's good to meet you," said Draygon, then he turned and strode off.

"That boy has a hard shell, if I've ever seen one," muttered Dean.

"Why do you say boy?" asked Temple, "How old is 'e?"

"He was fifteen at his first race, so 'e's nineteen."

"Oh, said Temple.

Chapter 9

Daris paced up and down the street, with the one working light. The sun beat down on his head, but he didn't care. He kicked all the rocks in his path as hard as he could. His face was screwed up in a scowl, which made him look fiercer then normal. A figure appeared at the end of the street, stopped, and stared down it. Daris did three more laps than stopped, facing away from the person. He whirled around, "If you don't get your hind out 'u here I'm 'onna beat the tar out 'o—," he stopped and stared into the calm face of Draygon McSqaw.

"What's goin' on?" asked Draygon, striding toward him.

"Nothin' much," said Daris.

Draygon stopped just in front of him and stared into his eyes.

"It's hard to get work when you have only one hand," he said quietly.

Daris stared back in surprise.

"Do you want a full-time job?" asked Draygon.

"Nobody would take me."

"I could teach you how to race cars with only one hand, and then the people I work for would take you. But it's tough work. You'd have to be prepared to sign a contract and keep it."

"Why would you do that for me? You haven't even met me."

"Dean Myles introduced us a week ago. But I would do it cause my Jesus would, and because I believe what my father used to tell me."

"What did he use to tell you?"

"That our greatest weakness can become our greatest strength."

"How?"

"I'll leave you to figure that out," Draygon turned and walked away.

He stopped at the end of the street and turned back, "I'll be in the parking lot of that church that's up for rent—five blocks down—with a car, every night. If you want to learn the job, meet me," then he was gone.

Daris stood still for a minute, then raced down the street into their sleeping alley. Dick started up, caught him and clamped his hand over Daris' mouth, "Shhh! Stop whippin' 'round like a maniac. He just went off to sleep."

Daris looked down at Darn's flushed face as he lay at full length on the ground, and then over at Dick, who had released his mouth.

"McSqaw just came by. He offered to teach me to race cars. I forgot I won't be earning any money for months if I except, and he'll either be dead or better by then. I'll let McSqaw know and ask if he's heard of any place that's hirin'."

"Then what's that cash stickin' out o' your pocket for?" asked Dick.

Daris looked down and pulled a wad of ten thousand dollars out of his pocket. A little paper fell to the ground. Dick picked it up and read the big, legible hand with small difficulty, "I will except some kind of payment in return, after you've won your first race. Not before. I keep my word. D. McSqaw."

"The fiend must 'ave snuck it when I was gawking at him—and I didn't even feel it!" exclaimed Daris.

"Thank God!" exclaimed Dick.

The two bent over Darn, lifted him up and bore him away.

Chapter 10

"I'm fine. I'm just tired," said Dick.

He was laying on his back in their sleeping alley. There were dark circles under his eyes and his cheeks were flushed.

"You've caught what Darn has, taking care of him so much," said Temple, who stood beside him.

The two of them were alone.

"I'm fine," repeated Dick, "Now go find some work. Maybe Dean needs some more writing done."

"Shank doesn't trust him," said Temple.

"Ignore Shank. Dean wouldn't have come back and fought with us if he wasn't a good guy. Now go. And don't tell any of the other boys about me, especially Daris. I don't want him to get scared and waste the money for Darn on me. When I'm just tired cause I stayed up with him the last several nights."

"Yes Dick," said Temple reluctantly.

He went out of their sleeping alley and started off down the alley with the one working light. He was just turning the corner, at the end of it, when he glanced back and saw Joshua and Johnathan entering it from the other end. He turned the corner quickly and pressed his back against the wall. Then the image of Dick, lying alone in their alley, came into his mind. They would find him. Temple took a deep breath and turned the corner again, this time facing them.

He folded his arms across his chest and called tauntingly, "Nana, nana, boo-boo! You can't catch me!"

They both grinned and darted forward. Temple turned and ran for his life.

They were faster and had much longer legs, so they quickly gained on him.

When they were almost upon him, he spun round and threw his fist into Johnathan's face. He fell backward and Temple came down on top, sinking his teeth into him. Joshua dragged Temple off and they both began beating him. But Temple saw with satisfaction that he'd broken Johnathan's nose. He tried to fight back like he knew Daris would. His right hand got pounded on, in just the wrong way, pain shot up his arm and he nearly passed out. Then he heard two heavy thuds—and both of his persecutors fell on top of him like dead weights. They were pulled off, and Temple found himself looking into the grinning face of Daris.

"Hey kid. What you doin' getting yourself into such a scrape," he said, helping Temple to his feet.

"I don't know. How did you knock them out like that?"

Daris held up his right forearm, he had capped the stump of his wrist with a metal-cup looking-thing.

"Found it in a trash heap. Draygon twisted and hammered it on for me." "Draygon McSqaw?"

"Yeah. He's giving me race car-driving lessons every night. But let me see that wrist you're bein' so dainty with, kid."

Temple carefully laid his hand in Daris.' Daris felt it and Temple fainted. Draygon

McSqaw caught him and raised him up in his arms.

"What are you doing here?" asked Daris.

"Trying to find you. I found your eldest brother unconscious in your alley. I took him to the hospital. I'll take this one there, too."

He turned and walked away. Daris clenched his teeth and followed him.

"Oh, will somebody wake me up from this nightmare," he muttered.

Draygon stepped on his foot, hard.

"Ow!"

"You're awake," stated McSqaw, calmly, "Let the hard stuff draw you closer to your Heavenly Father. It's how your pain can become your healing."

Chapter 11

ShawShank, Myles, Curtly—with his hand in a brace—and McSqaw sat in the hospital waiting room.

"What's the word on the hand," asked Dean, turning to Temple.

"It's messed up inside somehow so I'm never gonna be able to use it again," said Temp, "Unless I had a special surgery done, which we don't have the money for. But thankfully it's my left hand, not my right."

"If Dean actually cared about us, he'd pay for it," said Shank.

"He's already helping Draygon pay for Dick and Darn," said Shaw, "So maybe he's like us, not havin' that much money."

"A movie star and a race car driver ran out of money? Right," said Shank, in unbelief.

No one answered. The quiet soon became unbearable. Shank started tapping his feet and Dean began rolling his shoulders. A door at their right opened and Daris slowly entered the room. They all looked up expectantly. He walked over and threw himself into a seat without a word.

"Well?" asked Shank, after a minute.

"Is he ok?" asked Dean.

"What happened?" asked Temple.

Daris stared at them. Then he looked down at the floor and took a deep breath, "He's had heart problems ever since he was born. Every childhood illness, every cold messed with his heart somehow. He's taken the sickness worse than Darn, and of course it messed with his heart. He's had some kind of failure and the blood, or oxygen, or both, stopped goin' to the left side of his body and so his leg's gone black. At least I think that's what they said. I didn't understand so I could be all wrong. They're still workin' with him and his heart. But his leg's gonna have to come off. Darn's fine. He's gettin' better fast," and Daris nodded at the floor at which he still was staring.

There was a dead silence. Nobody moved. Finally, Temple whispered,

"How's Dick gonna take it?"

. . .

"Wohoo!!! This is awesome! Look at me!!! I lost one leg and gained two more!! This is great!!!" Dick was swinging up and down the street with only one light, on crutches.

ShawShank, Temple, Daris, Darn, Dean and Draygon were watching him.

"He's absolute nuts," muttered Shank.

"He deserves to be in an insane asylum, that's for sure," said Daris.

"He's so good," said Darn, "Oh, how I wish I could be like him."

Dick stopped in front of them, beaming. Daris, ShawShank and Temple stared at him incredulously.

Dick's grinning face softened into a quiet smile, "Really guys. I know you think I'm trying to pretend to be tough and not care. And yeah, I didn't want to lose my leg. It's different and a little hard. But yuh see, it's just not as big a deal for me as it would be to you. You all have ambitions. Temple's always wanted to be an author. Daris wants to race cars. Darn has his own quiet dream, that he doesn't want me to make public. I don't know about ShawShank—'cause they don't talk about themselves—but I bet they each have somethin' tucked away. And Dean and Draygon already have a career. I've never wanted one. I've never had any dreams. I'm content working at the gas station and I can do that on crutches."

"But isn't there *anything* else you want to do?" asked Darn.

"No," said Dick, simply, "Nothing."

He smiled brightly. Darn's eyes filled, he threw his arms around Dick's neck and held his brother tightly. "You're the best big brother in the world," he whispered.

"Big brother? You're triplets," said Shank.

"But I'm the eldest," grinned Dick, "By twenty seconds."

Chapter 12

Shaw stood alone in a deserted, trashed up alley. The sun was shining brightly on him— yet he felt cold, and very, very scared. He was afraid of something horrible that had happened to him before, but he didn't know what or why. Suddenly, his eyes focused on a figure approaching him. Something about it seemed familiar. It stopped just in front of him. A black mist covered its head, down over its eyes. But Shaw knew it must be Johnathan, because of the three scars that trailed down its cheek, to its jawline. Johnathan raised his arm, but Shaw couldn't move. He was frozen. Johnathan slugged him in the face. He felt no pain though he knew he should. As he fell backward the mist lifted off Johnathan's head, and Shaw saw that it was not Johnathan—but Dean. Dean with his sea green eyes and three scars trailing from his right eye, down to his jawline. Why? Shaw knew Dean didn't have any scars. Why was he thinking about scars? Dean had just hit him. He landed on his back with such impact that he rolled and rolled and rolled. It didn't hurt—but he kept rolling. Why didn't he stop? Why couldn't he stop? Shaw threw out his hands and stopped himself...

Shaw opened his eyes and sat up gasping.

He was sitting in the middle of a deserted, trashed up alley. The sun was shining down brightly on him—yet he felt cold and very, very scared. A figure entered the alley in front of him and came toward him. Shaw sprang to his feet—standing still and tense. It was Dean. Without any scars or black mist.

He grinned as he recognized Shaw, walked toward him and stopped just in front of him. Before Shaw could move, Dean swung a punch into the side of his head. Sending him reeling into the building on Dean's right. He hit with such impact that he passed out and crumpled to the ground. Dean had caught the knife aimed for Shaw's head with his right hand. He dropped it and clenched his sliced open hand. Johnathan,

Joshua, Arther and Jacob sauntered toward him from the other end of the alley.

"Nice catch," smirked Johnathan, "But don't worry. We'll take care of your little friend after we've dealt with you."

"Oh, I'm not worrying at all," responded Dean with his tantalizing smile, "Trust me."

"You know you can't win Myles," said Joshua, "We're not the same boys that rapped your mother. We're scarred men."

"No Joshua," said Dean, with that same smile, "You're two-year-olds who haven't gotten over themselves. Men live *with* their scars, not *in* them."

A muscle in Joshua's face twitched.

"You're not gonna win this one, Dean," growled Johnathan.

They encircled him. Dean was still smiling. He looked Johnathan straight in the eyes and said quietly, "I don't have to cause I've already proved that I'm stronger."

They sprang on him. Dean held his ground for a long time, ducking, dodging, pounding, ripping, and rolling. But the four boys used their knives and beat him down at last. Then they each took turns raping him. Johnathan was the last. After he finished, he staggered to his feet, pulled out his bloody knife and raised it. Then fell to the ground dead, a knife handle sticking out of his neck.

Joshua and the others sprang from the ground, their victim didn't move. He was unconscious. The boys looked back at Draygon McSqaw, who was running toward them, then down at Johnathan's stiffening body. Joshua took to his heels. Arther and Jacob followed their leader's example. Draygon reached the bodies, glanced at Johnathan then knelt beside Dean. Draygon ripped off his own shirt and tore it to shreds. He tightly bound up Dean's worst wounds. Then raised him in his arms like a baby, turned, and strode off down the street. Shaw stirred, opened his eyes, and slowly pushed himself to his feet. Putting his back to the wall and holding his head with both hands, he blinked and stared in front him. There was a good bit of blood on the ground. And there was Johnathan, lying on his face with the knife, sticking out of the back of his neck. Shaw shuddered, turned, and stumbled off down the street.

Chapter 13

Shank stood behind the counter inside a little, dirty gas station. Dick hobbled down one of the isles, with a spray bottle and a crutch in one hand and a rag and a crutch in the other.

"The bathrooms are quite clean," he declared with a grin, as he hopped around the counter, dropped to his knee, and put the spray bottle away. He struggled up to a standing position again and turned to Shank, "Where's Shaw been? He's supposed to be here with us."

Shank looked at Dick curiously, "Why do you ask when you know I'm not going to answer?"

"I like giving you the chance to trust somebody."

"I trust you."

"Then why don't you tell me?"

"Somebody could overhear us or find you and torcher you for the information."

"So, you trust me only up to a point."

Shank shrugged and turned away. The shop door opened, Shaw rushed in, dashed round the counter, and caught Shank by the arms, "Dean hit me!"

"He did?" Shank's eyes flashed and he spoke with quiet rage, "Where is he?"

"I don't know. But he hit me so hard it knocked me out. When I came to there was lots of somebody's blood on the ground. Johnathan was there—dead—with a knife in the back of his neck. And Dean was gone!"

"How did he know you were there? Weren't you hidden? What were you doing when he hit you?"

"I hid myself really well and fell asleep. Then I had this awful dream about Johnathan coming for me and turning into Dean— punching me and making me roll over and over. I must have really rolled cause I woke up in the middle of the street. Then Dean came toward me smiling. When he reached me, he punched me, and I fell against the wall beside us and passed out. Then I woke up, and there was the blood and Johnathan dead."

"Johnathan must have thrown the knife," said Dick, "Dean saw it, hit you out of the way, fought with him and was forced to kill him."

"Then why did he leave Shaw with the dead body. Why didn't he make sure he was ok and bring him to us himself," asked Shank, glaring at Dick.

"Maybe he got stabbed and had to hurry to hospital really fast or he would die," said Dick.

"Then he really only cares about himself."

"He could have known that he didn't hit Shaw hard enough to hurt him very bad."

"Yes. Let's go to the closest hospital and check," said Shaw quickly.

"There's too many maybe's and could haves. It can't be true," said Shank.

"It's the only thing that could be true!" cried Shaw.

"No it isn't," said Shank.

"Fine," said Shaw, "But *if* Dean had gotten hurt really bad for saving me, what should we do? Stand around and say he didn't, or go ask for him?"

"I'll mind the shop while you're gone," said Dick.

Shank glared at him and then followed his brother out.

. . .

"Did a boy of the name of Dean Myles just come here, very hurt?" asked Shaw walking up to the lady, at the front desk, in the hospital. Shank stood behind him.

"A boy of that name was just carried in here," said the lady.

"By who?" asked Shaw quickly, before the lady could continue.

"Another boy, who called himself Draygon McSqaw."

"Draygon McSqaw!" exclaimed ShawShank.

"Then was Dean very much hurt?" asked Shaw.

"He looked pretty bad. They took him to the ER."

"ShawShank over here," said Draygon, who had come out without their noticing.

"Thank you," said Shaw to the lady, then they hurried over to Draygon.

"Dean's in the ICU," said Draygon in an undertone, "Tell the gang. I've got to go turn myself in for killing Johnathan."

"You—," began Shaw.

Shank covered his brother's mouth.

"Go," he said to Draygon.

Draygon left. Shaw threw himself into his brother's arms.

"We need to pray for Dean," he whispered.

"And Draygon," said Shank.

Chapter 14

The Carmans, Curtly and ShawShank quietly entered the room where Dean lay. A thin sheet covered his body and bandages covered his face— all of it except his eyes. Those beautiful green eyes were glassy and clouded, like a muddy, green puddle. And he was hooked up to all sorts of things. He was tossing his head from side to side and mumbling inarticulately. Suddenly, he cried out distinctly, "Oh, forgive me! Please forgive me! I'm so sorry!"

Then fell back to mumbling. The gang looked at each other.

"It's just part of his ravings," said Dick.

"Will he ever heal from being so torn up down there," whispered Temple.

"The docs don't know," said Daris.

"And to think he had *that* happen for m—," Shaw was cut off by Dean's mumblings turning to clear talk.

"She was little. I know she was little. She had long hair; I can feel it. She was so skinny. I don't know. Everything's fuzzy. But I did it. They said I did. They found me in the act. She was so little. Johnathan's doing it. Mommy! Wake up! Come back! Heal. You must heal! Your body, it's—She was so little. Oh, come back. Come back! I'm so sorry. I'm so sorry! Forgive me. Heal! Don't die like mommy. I'm sorry, I really am sorry. Please, please forgive me! Forgive me! I'm so sorry!" and Dean began to weep pitifully, like a small child. "Forgive!" I'm sorry! So little! Sorry. Little. Forgive." And he sobbed and moaned. Burning tears filled Shaw's eyes.

"I'm so sorry. So sorry little one. Please, please forgive me. I'm so sorry," Dean begged, tears running out of his eyes. Shaw sprang forward, caught up Dean's hand and dropped to her knees beside his bed, "Oh, I do, Dean! I do! I forgave you, Dean, before I ever met you. I forgive you now. And I love you. I love you, Dean. So you can't die! Do you hear me!? I love you! I love you, Dean!"

Dean shook his head and began mumbling again. Shaw burst into tears; sobs shook her small body. Shank knelt down by her and wrapped her in his arms. The Carmans and Curtly exchanged glances. Dick nodded at the door and they quietly left the room. They stood out in the hall and stared at each other.

"Shaw's a—," Daris clamped his hand over Temple's mouth, "They didn't want us to know so let's not talk about it."

"Let's-uh," said Dick, "Um."

"Do you think there's enough evidence that they'll let Draygon off?" asked Darn.

"Oh yes," said Dick.

"I don't know," said Daris.

"Why wouldn't they?" asked Temple.

"They will," said Dick.

There was a long silence.

"How long will it take Dean to heal if he does live?" asked Temple.

"You heard the doc," said Dick, "They'll keep him here for a month and then I'm bettin' he'll get an apartment. And just be away from everybody, for at least another month."

There was another pause. Then Temple asked the question nobody else was willing to ask, "Do you think he will live?"

Everyone was quiet.

At last Darn said, "I don't know Temp."

"If love has anything to do with it—like people say," said Dick, "I think he will."

Chapter 15

The Carmans, ShawShank and Curtly stepped back and gazed up at the sign above the door of a little shop.

"Car-Man's mechanic shop," Dick read the words with a grin.

"I never knew you wanted to be a mechanic, Darn!" exclaimed Temple. Darn smiled his quiet smile.

"He never told anybody but us," Dick said, winking at Daris.

"Yes," said Darn, "And then Daris goes off and sneaks the secret—he promised never to reveal—to Draygon. And, of course, Draygon goes-has me learn some stuff-and then sets me up with my own shop."

"I didn't mean too," said Daris, "It just accidentally came out during one of my driving lessons from him and, of course, he acts on it. But, after he took him 'round to visit some other mechanics and their shops, he said Darn's got some real car genius and doesn't really need to learn anything. He said all Darn's got to do is look at a car and he knows what to do with it. And Darn's been doin' that since he was a baby."

Darn's eyes were dancing, and his face was all aglow. But he didn't say anything, just gazed up at his sign.

"And now ShawShank and I can help around here instead of at the gas station," said Dick.

"I was wondering if Shaw and Temple wouldn't like to come work in my department," said a familiar voice, close beside them.

They all spun round exclaiming, "Dean!!!"

"What are you doing here?" asked Dick, "It's not been two months quite."

"I got real bored in that stuffy, little apartment," said Dean, with the same old tantalizing smile. Three white scars trailed from his right eye down to his jaw line. "So I've been out a bit here and there. And today I just thought it would be nice to come and see how you all were doin.' What's this thing about workin' for Darn?"

Everyone turned to Darn.

"Draygon's got me a little mechanic shop. It's been my dream. Dick and maybe Shank are going to work for me. But what were you saying about Shaw? You want her and Temp to work with you?"

"Her?" Dean repeated, looking confused.

"Yes," said Shank stepping forward, "Shaw's a girl. But we can talk about it later cause it'll be hard."

Dean stared at him, then a look of understanding dawned in his face. He dropped his eyes, flushed, and turned away. But he turned back in a moment, "I'm ready if you are."

Shank looked hard into Dean's eyes. They looked like deep-but clear-green water. Dean looked back at him without flinching. The muscles in Shank's face relaxed and he held out his hand, "I forgive you. And I did what I did only to protect her. She was all I had."

Dean gripped Shank's hand hard. Shaw stepped up beside Shank and looked Dean straight in the eyes, "Thank you."

Dean looked back and then away, Shank and him released hands. There was a heavy silence.

"You wanted to offer Shaw and Temp a job situation?" asked Dick, at last. "Yes," said Dean, pulling himself together, "And that's *so* cool about your shop Darn."

"Thank you."

"Um," said Dean, "When the—my accident happened, I was coming to see if Temp and Shaw wanted to work for the production company that I work for. Temple's just so good at writing, especially stories. And—um. The company has been looking for some good singers which brought to mind—Shaw. I-uh, wasn't sure what you'd say but I thought I'd ask just in case you were interested. It won't pay that much, at least at first. I just thought it might be something you'd enjoy."

"I, I'd love to if they'd take me," said Temple, his eyes lighting up, "I mean, I'm only fifteen. But I'd love to if they'd take me."

"Oh, they will, trust me. We're pretty low on good script writers. They'll love to have you. It's about your talent, not your age."

"Thank you. I'll come."

"I'll watch out for him, Daris, I promise," and Dean turned to Shaw.

"Do you really think I'm a *good* singer?" she asked.

"Better than me. And they say I'm the best they have."

Shaw looked into Shank's face, questioningly. Shank looked at her, then turned to Dean, "You'll protect her, too?"

Dean flushed and answered quietly, "With my life."

Shank looked back at Shaw and nodded.

Shaw turned to Dean, "I'll come."

Dean looked down, then up at Darn, "Will you show me around your place?"

Darn smiled and led the way inside.

Chapter 16

The stars shown down brightly on ShawShank as they walked slowly along an empty street, that had all of its lights intact. It was dark time. They were halfway down it when Shaw turned, grabbing Shank by the arms, and looked into his face. They stared at each other in silence.

"I'm finally gonna be a singer," said Shaw, at last, "Aren't you glad for me?"

Shank's face softened into a tender smile, "You don't know how much."

"And I'm going to be known there as the girl I am. I can't act like a boy and live my dream, Shank."

"You're right. And I wouldn't ask you to. I'll trust you to Dean."

"You trust him now?"

"He endured what he did to you, for you—without knowing. And that takes a real man."

"How do you think he's gotten over it so quickly?"

"I don't think he's gotten over it. But I think he's getting through it so well *only* because he has Jesus."

"Or rather, Jesus has him."

"Yes."

Shaw leaned into Shank and laid her head on his shoulder. They were quiet for a while.

Then Shaw lifted her head, "You have a dream too, Shank. I know you do. Mine's going to be fulfilled now and I'm going to be protected in it, so it's ok to follow yours. Won't you share it with me? Can't I help you find it? Can't we serve God together with what he's put inside us? What is your ambition?"

Shank took a deep breath, "You really wanna know?"

"Please."

He stepped back; she released his arms.

"Sing me a song."

Shaw looked at him quizzically, then stared at the ground. She raised her head and began in her lovely alto. And, as she sang, Shank began to dance. He had perfect flow and rhythm. It was beautiful. And Shaw laughed in wonder as she sang,

"She's fifteen and he's barely driving a car

She's got his ring and he's got the keys to her heart

It's just a matter of time

They'll spread their wings and fly

"Like two sparrows in a hurricane

Trying to find their way

With a head full of dreams

And faith that can move anything

"They've heard it's all uphill

But all they know is how they feel

The world says they'll never make it

Love says they will

"There's a baby crying and one more on the
way
There's a wolf at the door
With a big stack of bills they can't pay
The clouds are dark, and the wind is high
But they can see the other side

"Like two sparrows in a hurricane
Trying to find their way
With a head full of dreams
and faith that can move anything

"They've heard it's all uphill
But all they know is how they feel
The world says they'll never make it
Love says they will

"She's eighty-three and barely driving a car
She's got his ring and he's got the keys to
her heart
It's just a matter of time
They'll spread their wings and fly

"Like two sparrows in a hurricane
Trying to find their way
With a head full of dreams
And faith that can move anything

"They've heard it's all uphill
But all they know is how they feel
The world says they'll never make it
Love says they will"

[*Two Sparrows In A Hurricane*, by Ms. Tanya Tucker]

Shank stopped in front of her and, with a little bow, held out his hand. She took it and he swung her around, in step, as she sang:

"Like two sparrows in a hurricane
Trying to find their way
With a head full of dreams
And faith that can move anything

"They've heard it's all uphill
But all they know is how they feel
The world says they'll never make it
Love says they will"

They stopped staring into each other's faces.

"The world has said we won't many times," said Shank.

"And our God, who is love, says we will," said Shaw.

Then ShawShank fell into each other's arms and held each other tight.

"Um."

They both jumped, released each other, and turned toward Dean.

"Why do you always have to scare us like that," asked Shank.

"I'm sorry. I don't mean to. But I've been worried about how quiet the Scar gang has been. You said you guys haven't seen an inch of them since Johnathan's death. That must mean they'er planning somethin' big. I think we should be keeping together as much as possible, or at least within call.

So I was wondering if you would join me and the other boys in following Daris, to his driving lessons with Draygon. Daris'll be mad at us if we tell him, but when he's alone like that it's the perfect time to hurt 'im. So I was wondering if we could sneak after him to make sure he gets there, ok. It's only five blocks from our street."

"If we bring Dick, Daris is sure to find out cause of his thumping," said Shank.

"We'll carry him if we have to," said Dean.

Shank looked at Shaw, "Ready?"

"Ready."

Shank nodded at Dean and they followed him into the night.

Chapter 17

Daris arrived at the parking lot and looked around. It was empty.

"Draygon's always here before me," he muttered and squinted his keen eyes in every direction. Then he clenched his hand, walked out of the parking lot, passed the church and up the next street, peering into every alley it had. He stopped as he looked down the third alley. There was a car parked in the middle of it. The car Draygon always brought. It was on. Every window it had was broken. Its lights showed up the body in laying front of it. The mangled form of Draygon McSqaw. Daris stood frozen. Then ran toward it. Joshua, Arthur, Jacob and massive Dunce sprang out of the shadows in front of it. Dawn, Dara, Michael and Eric stepped out at his left. James, John, and Caleb at his maimed right. And Sheryl, Sherry, Jeff and Tom behind him.

Joshua smiled at him, "Come to find the hero you can't do without? We've had a big score to pay off with McSqaw for a long time. But he capped his doom by gettin' between us and you. And then he threw the body of my best man on top o' that. So we just ran him over with the car he used to help you. But enough about him. He's been paid his cash. It's your turn now."

The Scar gang closed in around Daris. Daris held Joshua with his dark blue eyes, a grim smile played about his lips and he made a fist with his left hand, "Just you make sure to pay me the same amount, and I'll make sure to make it the biggest debt I can."

Joshua's smile vanished and his face became hard as rock, "Pay' im boys."

And they all rushed on Daris. Daris swung his metal capped stump at Joshua. Joshua caught it and swung his other hand but Daris caught that. Then they closed in a deadly wrestling match. But why hadn't he been torn to shreds from the sides and behind? Daris knew he couldn't let himself think about it. He had to focus everything he had on Josh. But Shank's well known fighting laugh, Dick's grunts and Temple's squeaky throat noises let him know that he was not alone. And it was a good thing to know. Dean's charge had taken the scar gang by surprise. But they recovered themselves in a moment and lashed back.

Dean got locked up in a hopeless fight with the giant Dunce. Jacob, Dunce's "little" brother, saw it. And not being engaged with anyone, drew his knife. With glittering eyes, he made for him. Shank saw him, danced Sherry dizzy, broke her nose and leapt for Dean. He tackled him away from Dunce, to the ground, with himself on top. Darn, from his position on the ground, yanked Jacob's legs out from under him just before he reached them. But Dunce's huge fist came down, with its full strength, on Shank's back. There was a loud snap, and he knew no more. Dick had turned his crutches into weapons of war. He managed to separate Daris and Joshua and got beat to a pulp for it. Shaw saw Joshua using Dick's head as a hammer on the asphalt street. She rammed her fist into the right side of Dara's lower jaw. It made a terrible cracking sound, Dara staggered and almost passed. By the time she could see again Shaw had both arms round Joshua's neck, squeezing with all her strength. Arthur pounced on her. Dara joined him and they tried to pull her arms off, but they were like twisted-together steel. Joshua was slugging her in the face, but it didn't help. Arthur finally came round and hit her in the side of the head. She passed out and Dara and he were able to wrench her off their leader. Then they started working on her. Dean had rolled from under Shank, pulled him to the side, out of the fight and then dived back into it. He saw Shaw's little, white, bare foot, sticking out from under the two miniature hulks. Dean flew on them and broke both their necks. He raised Shaw in his arms, carried her over and laid her down by Shank. Then sprang back into action. Darn was still struggling with Jacob, but his strength was wearing out and the, man's knife was coming, every slash, closer to making a lethal stab. He twisted the knife out of Darn's hands for the last time and shot it down toward his side when his head and Daris' metal stump made connection. It threw him sideways, stunning him. Daris hit him thrice more and he passed out. Daris raised his eyes to see Temple, engaged with Sheryl, Sherry, and Dawn.

And Joshua, recoiling with his knife raised, was about to make a mortal stroke at his unsuspecting victim. Daris whipped out his knife and released, with the quickness of a snake. Joshua toppled onto Dawn, his knife sinking into her neck and they both dropped dead.

Sherry screamed—everything paused.

Despite the miniature victories, the Scar gang was beating the boys down with their superior strength and numbers. But when they saw their leader—the only one ever able to hold them together—twisted up on top of Dawn, with the handle of a knife sticking out from between his eyes, they each - separately - turned and ran.

Daris reeled to his feet. "I'm going to get an ambulance," he yelled to no one in particular, and made for Draygon's car.

Reaching it, he got in, drove backward, turned it and shot away.

"Where did he say he was going?" asked Temple, falling to his knees.

"To get an ambulance cause we don't have phones," slurred Darn, rolling to his hands and knees, "If he ever becomes a racer though, he'll never drive as fast as he will tonight."

"Or as wobbly," muttered Dean, dropping on his rear.

Chapter 18

Shank lay on his belly, in a white bed, in a small, white hospital room. His face was screwed up and he was muttering between his clenched teeth, "God. God, if You—if You are mocking me. Then-then I'll-,"

"Praise You," said Dean, stepping into the room and quietly seating himself, on the floor, by Shank.

Shank glared at him.

Dean looked back, steadily, "I'll praise You, God. I'll say your ways are beautiful. And that you are good."

"If He's mocking me, He's not good," said Shank, his voice quivering with anger.

"He is, Shank. He's always good. No matter what He's doing. Shadrach, Meshach and Abed-nego said, *even if He does not deliver us* from the furnace of blazing fire, we are not going to serve or worship your gods or your image.' And Job said, 'Though He slay me, I will hope in Him.'"

"But He let me have it and then snatched it away. Being a dancer has always been my dream, but I always held it back. I was Shaw's guardian, nothing else. I was not allowed to think of myself unless she was cared for. And I did it. She was finally going to live her dream. And when she asked me what mine was, I felt like God was saying, 'It's time. Seek your dream now. I'm calling you. Come dance with me, Shank.' And then He goes and paralyzes me from the waist down. I can't stand it! I won't! He has no right to mock me. If He wants to play that game I'll play it with Him and I-", Shank choked and was silent.

Dean's eyes were full of tears, "Oh Shank. I don't know. I don't have the answers. But I know that our God is good. Shank, I lost everything when mom got raped. I took everything when I raped Shaw. But God let me give everything when I was raped—by the boys who rapped my mom—for Shaw. And I mean *everything*. Cause it's all gone after you go through that. Everything you thought you were, everything you thought you had. It's gone. But I can see now that the process He brought me through—lose, take, give—is beautiful. It's good. Because not only did He save me for eternal life, He let me be redeemed here. He let what I did be redeemed. He let Shaw be redeemed. And you gotta admit—that's beauty. And you're right, I can't see the good of you bein' paralyzed. I can't see the good of Draygon living threw being run over only to die here. And I definitely can't see the good in Daris goin' to jail for life, for saving Temp from Josh. When I go scot free for the same thing, except that I killed two."

"So they did condemn him?"

"Yeah. He's done some things in the past as I'm sure you know, being his buddy, so he has a bad rep. And Dick said his judge and a few of the jury have a thing or two against him, so they condemn him as guilty."

They were silent for a few minutes.

"Anyway," said Dean, standing up, "We can't see it. But it's there somewhere. Cause our God is good and we're His children."

"Why didn't Shaw come?"

"She was so upset by the word on you that I asked her to try to calm down before she came in. I'll go see if she's ready."

Shank closed his eyes and pressed his lips together. When Shaw came in, alone, he smiled up at her as brightly as he could. Though his lips were quivering. She threw herself on her knees beside him and burst into tears, hiding her face in his pillow. He pressed his lips to her hair and murmured shakily, "The world's saying it again isn't it?"

Shaw's head moved but she didn't speak.

"But our God, who is love, is saying we will," he whispered.

Chapter 19

In Car-Man's mechanic shop, in a small back room, in his wheelchair, Shank sat bending over the accounts.

"I detest math. Curse you, horrid numbers," he muttered.

"But praise God for the money they stand for," said Dean, cheerily,

entering the room.

"Umph," said Shank, "And what are you jumping out of your pants for?" "Draygon can leave the hospital on the fifteenth."

"The fifteenth? —Wait…That's the day we all went in. That means he's been in that dreadful place a year."

"It's not dreadful. Hospitals are very good for when you get wounded, especially like him, and don't have family to care for you. I just wouldn't want to stay in one a year. But they were sure he'd die when he went in, so I guess it's an improvement."

"Not really. How long will he have to be in rehab?"

"You know McSqaw. He's done all his rehab in the hospital. Crazy man."

"Ok. What else? Somebody found their brain and gonna try Daris' case again?"

"No, said Dean sadly, "Nothing that good."

"What then?"

"Oh, um. I—I wanted to ask you-uh."

"What?"

"Um. Something I'm not sure if you'll like. And if you don't, just say so and I'll never ask again. I don't want it-if it'll hurt you in anyway."

"Want what?" asked Shank, cocking an eyebrow.

"Oh, just—just, um."

Shank eyed Dean grimly. Dean looked at him, dropped his eyes, then looked up and blurted, "Permission to ask your sister for her hand in marriage. If you agree with me that I'm not worthy of her or if you wouldn't like me too—if it'd hurt you at all in the slightest way—make you feel uncomfortable or farther away from her, say so. I'll never speak of it again. But I promise it won't change anything. We'll still be with you and the gang after work, and still sleep in the same alley—everything. But please say what you really think."

Dean flushed up to the roots of his hair after this speech and rolled his shoulders.

Shank stared hard at him, then grinned broadly, "Finally. that took you forever. I started to wonder if you'd ever ask. Of course you have my permission and my greatest hopes into the bargain. I've wanted you to marry her since the day we saw you in the hospital, after your accident. You'll take good care of her. And be to her what I can't be now. Yes. I'm am very, very glad you asked."

Dean's face expressed the shock he felt. Shank laughed.

"There's only one thing, Dean."

Dean nodded quickly.

"I think you two should sleep alone in our alley and the rest of us-old bachelors-sleep on our street. Just for conveniences' sake."

Dean laughed nervously.

Shank eyed him quizzically, "Ok. What else? You got something else in there and you know it."

"It's just-uh."

"Another "just"—hu. Well, my sister's not a "just," you know."

"No, she's not," agreed Dean quickly, "It's just—do you think she cares about me at all?"

The corners of Shank's mouth twitched, "Well, I guess you'll have to go find out, won't you?"

"Thank you," said Dean, and he started to go out.

"Hey, Dean," said Shank.

"Yeah."

"I found out what good there is in this," and Shank pointed to his legs, "I was able to give them up to save Shaw, one last time."

"Save Shaw," repeated Dean, "But—from what?"

"A broken heart."

. . .

Shaw stood, on the empty stage-with its curtains down, of the production company she, Temple, and Dean, worked for. She was wearing a beautiful, sea blue dress and her lovely brown hair fell round her shoulders. She was rubbing her bare foot across the floor and singing softly, with tears glistening in her eyes:

"She's fifteen and he's barely driving a car
She's got his ring and he's got the keys to her heart
It's just a matter of time
They'll spread their wings and fly

"Like two sparrows in a hurricane
Trying to find their way
With a head full of dreams
And faith that can move anything"

She pressed her hand over her mouth to stifle the sob rising up in her throat and the tears slipped down her cheeks. But someone who'd come in behind her took up the song and continued it in his rich tenor:

"They've heard it's all uphill
But all they know is how they feel
The world says they'll never make it
Love says they will"

She turned and looked at Dean.

He gazed at her then dropped to one knee, "Shaw, I want to do it right this time. Would you care to give me the chance?"

She dropped to her knees and looked him straight in the eyes, "I love you, Dean, but I think I need to remain single for Shank. I love him so much and he's—he's been so good to me. Even though I'm older than him, by six seconds, he's always taken care of me. I need to take care of him now."

"We both can—together. Cause he's given me his permission and really seemed glad about it. The only difference there'll be in our lives is us sleeping alone in our alley while the gang sleeps on our street."

Shaw stared at him, "But I can't have any babies. You'd be so good with babies."

"But I can't either."

Shaw stared at him again. Her eyes opened wide, then filled with unshed tears. Dean opened his arms, "I love you, Shaw."

She threw herself into his arms and they held each other tightly.

Chapter 20

Darn entered McSqaw's hospital room. Draygon was sitting on the side of his bed. His face was pale, so the scars that crisscrossed it showed up well. The short stump of his right arm stuck out of his shirtsleeve. He rose and held out his left hand.

Darn took it with his left, "I asked the others to let me pick you up, alone. I want to take you to my shop before you see them. Will you come?"

Draygon nodded and followed him out of the room.

. . .

Darn led Draygon into the back room of his shop.

"Please sit down in that chair."

Draygon sat. Darn went to one of his cabinets, took a key out of his pocket and opened it. He reached in and brought out a metal arm, just the size of the one Draygon had lost.

"I made this for you. It has computer technology in it so the hand can anticipate how to move by the way you move your arm. I made a recharging system which you'll probably have to use every month. Do you mind taking off your shirt?"

Draygon did. Darn screwed and strapped the arm to Draygon's stump. He put another strap from the front of the arm, round Draygon's neck to the back of the arm. Then another round the stump, across his chest and back then around the stump again. Then he brought out a skintight, long sleeved, black shirt. And one, out of a pair, of gloves he used when working on cars. He had Draygon put them on. Then stepped back and looked at him.

"Why did you do this for me?" Draygon asked.

Darn answered quietly, "Because I believe that our greatest weakness can become our greatest strength."

The muscles in Draygon's face tightened.

"You loved him, too," said Darn.

Then he looked away, "I miss him."

Draygon held out his metal right hand, Darn took it with his right.

Draygon spoke quietly, "I do too."

Chapter 21

Draygon finished shaking the hands of ShawShank, Dick and Dean.

Then he looked around, "Where's Temple?"

The others glanced round quickly.

"I don't know," said Dean.

"Come to think of it," said Dick, "We haven't seen him since Darn left to get you."

"And it's not workday," said Darn.

"There he is," said Draygon, as Temple whipped round the corner of their street and came flying toward them.

Something in his eyes made them all start forward exclaiming, "What's the matter?!"

But Draygon reached him first and he collapsed into him, gasping for breath, "A wild man! ... With a bushy beard and long hair! ... Chasing me!!!"

They all looked up as the man of Temple's description raced round the corner toward them. Draygon put Temple aside and stood still. The man came on like a maniac, not slackening his pace for an instant. He hurled himself at Draygon, and Draygon swung. His metal fist and the metal capped stump of Daris met—and Daris was thrown flat on his back. It quite knocked the wind out of him. Draygon was on his knees, by his side, in a moment and helped him to his feet. Then caught him to his chest in a tight embrace.

"Get your metal arm off me! You're smushing me," Daris gasped.

Draygon released him.

"There! I can breathe!"

But he was instantly caught from behind and before, by Dick and Darn and smushed again.

"There!" he said, as they let go, "Op, not there!" as Dean and Temple laid hold on him.

"There! Finally!"

But he was caught round the waist and pulled into Shank's lap, while Shaw fell to her knees and threw her arms round him in front.

"Uh, definitely not there."

They released him, he stood up and shook himself.

"How did you get out!" exclaimed Dick, "Did you escape!?"

Daris winked at Temple.

"No. Temp's been using all the friends he's made, in the production company, and all their contacts. They finally got the case retried and here I am."

Everyone turned to Temple.

"The surprise and the joke was Daris' idea," said Temple, nodding quickly,

"I just did what he told me."

"Wow," said Dick, "God is so good."

"I'm so glad to have you back," said Darn.

"It's actually not that bad seein' all your faces again," Daris grinned.

"But your's is a little bad to look at," said Shaw, "You're going to have to shave and cut your hair before my wedding."

"Your wedding? Dean finally asked?"

"I know," said Shank, "Took him a whole year."

"I think we should thank God right now," said Dean, "Dick, will you lead us?"

"Sure."

They all bowed their heads and shut their eyes.

"Dear Jesus, I—we—thank You!"

. . .

A clean shaven, military hair styled Daris, and Temple took their seats in the hospital waiting room.

"We're here," said Temple, "Now tell me what this is all about."

Daris stared into Temple's light brown eyes and then said, "While I was in jail, I earned all the money I could. Draygon added to it, and it's just enough to pay for the surgery that'll enable you to use your hand again."

Temple turned away and sat perfectly still. Daris was silent, then tapped him on the shoulder,

"Everything ok, kid?"

Temple turned back around and threw his arms round Daris' neck, smushing him yet again.

"Thank you," he whispered.

Chapter 22

It was dusk in the side street with the one working light. Dick stood on his foot, leaning on his crutches, and holding his small, well-worn Bible before him. A scar ran from his right ear, over his nose, to the other ear.

Dean and Shaw stood before him. Shaw had a two-inch scar on her left cheek and Dean had Johnathan's three scars.

Darn, Daris and Temple stood together. Temple's scar ran from his right temple, straight down to his jaw line.

Scars criss crossed themselves all over Daris' face and Darn had a long scar across his forehead.

Shank sat a little apart from them in his wheelchair, a scar ran from his right temple across his face to his left jawbone.

McSqaw stood three feet away from him, with his arms folded across his chest and scars crisscrossing themselves over his face.

All of them, even the bride and groom, were wearing white T-shirts, leather jackets and Tena shoes. Excepting that ShawShank were bare foot and Draygon wore a long, skintight, black shirt, one glove, and no jacket.

"Do you Dean Myles, take Shaw as your wife? To have and to hold—for better or for worse—as long as you both shall live?" asked Dick gravely.

"I do," said Dean firmly.

"And do you, Shaw, take Dean Myles as your husband? To have and to hold—for better or for worse—as long as you both shall live?"

"I do," said Shaw clearly.

"Then you have become one flesh. What God has joined together, let no man separate," and Dick closed the Bible, "Dean, kiss'er."

All the boys looked away. Dean turned to Shaw, took her face in his hands and bent

down toward her. Shaw tilted up her face.
And they kissed. When they were done,
16-year-old Temple stepped forward and
began to sing in his clear voice,

> "Young man, up on the hillside,
> teaching new ways.
> Each word winning them over,
> each heart a kindled flame."

Then 18-year-old Daris:

> "Old man, watching from the outside,
> guarding their prey.
> Threatened by the voice of a paragon
> leading their lambs away,
> leading them far away."

18-year-old Darn:

> "Nobody knew His secret ambition,
> Nobody knew His claim to fame.
> He broke the old rules steeped in tradition,
> He tore the holy veil away."

18-year-old Dick:

> "Questioning those in powerful position.
> running to those who called His name.
> Nobody knew His secret ambition
> was to give His life away."

20-year-old Draygon:

> "His rage, shaking the temple,
> His word to the wise.
> His hand healing on the seventh day,
> His love wearing no disguise."

19-year-old Dean:

> "Some say death to the radical
> he's way out of line.
> Some say praise be the miracle
> God sends a blessed sign.
> A blessed sign for troubled times."

17-year-old Shaw:

> "Nobody knew His secret ambition,
> Nobody knew His claim to fame.
> He broke the old rules steeped in tradition,
> He tore the holy veil away."

17-year-old Shank:

> "Questioning those in powerful position
> running to those who called His name.
> Nobody knew His secret ambition
> was to give His life away."

[*Secret Ambition* by Mr. Michael W. Smith]

"I've been wondering," said Temple, with contracted brows, "Ever since Shaw started teaching us that song—how we can ever be like Him? Cause the Bible says we're supposed to be. But—He was so good! I mean, all of us have dreams, ambitions, or no ambition, like Dick, or dreams that have been dashed, like Shank. I'm a script writer. Shaw's a singer. Dean's an actor. Darn's a mechanic. Daris just won his first race so he's like Draygon. And Dick and Shank work for Darn. There's nothing in all that. We're all just doing or not doing what we want to do. *His* secret ambition was to give His life away. That was His *dream*-what He *lived* for. And He had claim to the biggest fame. We don't have any. Yet He's the one living to die. What are we doing to be like Him? What can we do to be like Him? Should we all go be missionaries? I don't want to at all. I want to write. I love to write! But isn't it wrong of me? Shouldn't I go and try to save people's souls from going to hell?"

"Oh, Temp!" exclaimed Dick, "No! God is the only one who can save souls and He'll call you to that if He wants to use you like that. But He can save souls through your stories. And if He put that love for story in your heart, He's calling you to use it. He'll let you know if you go too far—He's your loving father. But He put that talent inside of you to use—to double and triple—not to hide in the ground, like the wicked slave in the Bible, and give back to Him at the end of your life. Saying, 'Here's what you gave me, I wouldn't use it cause I didn't want you to take it for yourself.' No! And you're right—He didn't give us the dream of giving up our lives for others. We lay them down in the little things, every day. We just weren't called to the big."

Temple took a deep breath, "Thank you."

"Now Shaw," Shank said, "We did what you asked us to, now sing us a real wedding song."

Shaw gazed at her brother, "I will sing for you. But it'll be for Shank and a song of my choosing."

Dean held out his hand, Shaw took it and, as they danced, she sang,

"Lookin' back
On the memory of
The dance we shared
Beneath the stars above

"For a moment
All the world was right
How could I have known
That you'd ever say goodbye?

"And now, I'm glad I didn't know
The way it all would end
The way it all would go
"Our lives are better left to chance
I could have missed the pain
But I'da had to miss
The dance

"Holding you
I held everything
For a moment wasn't I the king?

"But if I'd only known how the king would
fall
Hey, who's to say
You know, I might have changed it all

"And now, I'm glad I didn't know
The way it all would end
The way it all would go

"Our lives are better left to chance
I could have missed the pain
But I'da had to miss
The dance
"It's my life
It's better left to chance
I could have missed the pain
But I'da had to miss
The dance"

[*The Dance* by Mr. Garth Brooks]

Shank had covered his face with one hand, and silent tears were running down Shaw's face as she and Dean stopped in front of her "little" brother. She knelt down, put her hands on his legs and looked up at him:

"I could have missed the pain
But I'da had to miss
The dance"

Shank caught up Shaw's hands in his, revealing a tearstained face, red eyes, and quivering lips.

"I'm glad I didn't know," he whispered, "Our lives are better left to God."

"But you could have missed the pain of finally realizing your dream only to have it shattered."

"I wouldn't have missed that dance for double the pain."

Shaw bowed her head in Shank's lap, and he bowed his over her. There was dead silence for a while. Then Shank sat upright quickly rubbing his arm across his eyes. And Shaw stood up and shook herself. Everyone looked around at each other and then dropped their eyes. There was an awkward silence.

Daris broke it, "Um. Uh. Hey! Temple, ever come up with a name for our gang? I mean, if you wanted, we could probably be called the new Scar gang with all our ugly faces."

"I don't think we could," said Dick.

"No," said Darn.

"Why not?" asked Daris.

"I just don't think so," said Dick.

"It wouldn't stick," said Darn.

"Why not?" asked Dean.

"Maybe," said Draygon, "Because we haven't let our scars define us."

They were all quiet.

"The people who know about us have already named us. And it's stickin' around this part of town pretty good," said Temple, "I don't know if we'll be able to shake it."

"What is it?" asked Daris.

Temple smiled quietly, "The McSqaw gang."

"GREATER LOVE HAS NO MAN THAN THIS, THAT ONE LAY DOWN HIS LIFE FOR HIS FRIENDS."   JOHN 15:13

THE END